This is a bitter, difficult and brilliant play. Wallace Shawn's world is a purgatorial no man's land where men and women, living and partly living, breathe the heady poisonous air of culture and its discontents. —*The* (London) *Sunday Times*

In a series of exquisite cross-cut monologues, there emerges a picture of patrician sensibility and snobbery . . . that really scares the shit out of the audience . . . The event has already generated a lot of excitement and has all the markings of a theatrical breakthrough. —JOHN ·   orker

Strange name and e.   *ms its way into the cons*   *is over . . . Unsettling, o*   *. .e fastidiousness of the language and the detached tone in which horrific events are recounted exert a hypnotic power.* —*Time Out*

Wallace Shawn is the Obie award–winning author of *Aunt Dan and Lemon, Marie and Bruce, A Thought in Three Parts, The Fever,* and other plays. A noted stage and screen actor, he and André Gregory wrote the screenplay for and performed in *My Dinner with André.* Mr. Shawn lives in New York.

THE

DESIGNATED

MOURNER

THE

DESIGNATED

MOURNER

Wallace Shawn

The Noonday Press

Farrar, Straus and Giroux

New York

The Noonday Press
A division of Farrar, Straus and Giroux
19 Union Square West, New York 10003

Copyright © 1996 by Wallace Shawn
All rights reserved
Distributed in Canada by Douglas & McIntyre Ltd.
Printed in the United States of America
Designed by Cynthia Krupat
First published in 1996 by Faber and Faber, England
First American edition published in 1996 by Farrar, Straus and Giroux
First Noonday edition, 1997

The Library of Congress has catalogued the hardcover edition as follows:
Shawn, Wallace.
  The designated mourner / Wallace Shawn.
    p.   cm.
    ISBN 0-374-13822-2
    1. Man-woman relationships—Drama.   2. Fathers and daughters—
Drama.   I. Title.
PS3569.H387D47   1996
812'.54—dc20   98-17844

Profound thanks and a big hug to the D.A.A.D., Berlin,
and Joachim Sartorius

to my darling, D. E.,

and all the other poets and writers

THE

DESIGNATED

MOURNER

THE DESIGNATED MOURNER

was first performed at the Royal National Theatre

in the Cottesloe auditorium on 18 April 1996

with the following cast:

J A C K—*Mike Nichols*

J U D Y—*Miranda Richardson*

H O W A R D—*David de Keyser*

Directed by David Hare

Designed by Bob Crowley

Lighting by Rick Fisher

Sound by Freya Edwards

CHARACTERS

JACK

JUDY

HOWARD

Jack is older than Judy.
Howard is older than Jack.

PART ONE

JACK *(to the audience)*

The designated mourner. I am the designated mourner. I have to tell you that a very special little world has died, and I am the designated mourner. Oh yes, you see, it's an important custom in many groups and tribes. Someone is assigned to grieve, to wail, and light the public ritual fire. Someone is assigned when there's no one else.

Christ, you know, I remember so clearly the moment—when *was* that?—years ago—when someone was saying, "If God didn't like assholes, He wouldn't have made so many of them," and the person who was saying it looked right at me as he said it—ha ha ha—

I think someone asked me, "Say, are you all right?" And I said, you know, "Oh, it doesn't matter. It doesn't bother me. I mean, I'm fine, really." By the way, do you remember when people used to say that all the time? "I'm fine, really"? "I'm fine really"? Ha ha ha—I must admit, it was an expression I always absolutely hated, but anyway, you know, we all used it—aha ha ha—

I remember saying to Judy, "I don't sort of understand this need you have to look for beauty in subtler things. Look at your own hand—look at your hand, the plate, the cake, the table . . ."

JUDY *(to the audience)*

I guess the search for more refined forms of punishment never comes to an end. After all, there are so many ways that life can be squeezed out of a human body. "Can a method be found that is more in keeping with the essential sweetness of our human nature?" a rather cruel queen once plaintively asked, or so it is said.

I loved him so much, it was a kind of torture. Every morning, waiting, watching his face, in those squirming long moments of sleep and half-sleep as he turned and stretched—I sat there beside him, my hand beside him not touching him, and pain would fill up my body inch by inch, as if someone were pouring it out of a pitcher.

JACK *(to the audience)*

You see, I think we ought to be precise about facts—I mean, very, very precise about historical facts. Or I mean, for God's sake, let's *try* to be. Or I mean, for God's sake, let's *pretend* to be. Or something, anyway. Well, at any rate . . . At any rate, there are those who believe that it was a columnist for a newspaper called *The New York Sun* who, in 1902, first coined that wonderful pair of neatly matching phrases "highbrow" and "lowbrow."

JUDY

I watched him wake up, the squirming stilled, touched his face, his neck, his mouth, kissed him, one hand lying deep in his hair, oily and thick like a bucket full of worms. The one thing he never would say—the word he couldn't stand: love. I love you.

JACK

A "highbrow" was a person who liked the finer things—you know, saving the Rembrandt from the burning building, rather than the baby or the fried chicken or whatever—while a "lowbrow" was someone who you might say liked to take the easy way in the cultural sphere—oh, the funny papers, pinups—you know, cheap entertainment.

JUDY

There are ideas that are almost like formalized greetings. Everyone agrees with them, but we keep repeating them anyway, all day long. Everyone keeps saying, for example, "Human motivation is very complex." But if you stop and think about it, you have to admit that human motivation is *not* complex, or it's complex only in the same sense that the motivation of a fly is complex. In other words, if you try to swat a fly, it moves out of the way. And humans are the same. They step aside when they sense something coming, about to hit them in the face. Of course you do see the occasional exception—the person who just stands there and waits for the blow.

I love silence, the beauty of silence. The shadows of trees. Japanese monasteries buried in snow, surrounded by forest. Loneliness, death, in the dark forest. But my life was different, a different way: A city. People. Concerts. Poetry.

Altogether, I was lucky—one of the few—because I paid a little price for the things that I thought. I paid a price, so my life was not nothing, my life had something in it.

JACK

All human beings have a need to hear stories, and a pretentious fraud I knew in school even used to say that stories are actually "as necessary as food." I *hated* that. But do you know, it's true? If people don't dream at night, they go insane, and by day, they need stories—it's just that simple. Some people like to get their stories from gossip, and some people like to get them from novels or plays, but personally I've always liked newspapers the best. The stories in newspapers are brief, they're varied, and, every once in a while, you get to read about someone you know—a friend or acquaintance suddenly pops up.

Incidentally, have you ever noticed the way that people are always asking, as if there would be a new answer each time, "How can this have happened? How can *that* have happened?! Why, it seems impossible!" et cetera. And yet, actually, the answer to those questions is always the same. You remember I was mentioning God a moment ago? Well, that reminded me of something an old acquaintance of mine always used to say when people said things like that. He always used to say, "God's not in His heaven. And all's not right with the world." Aha ha ha—aha ha ha ha. But to me, you see—well, he always seemed to me to have the right idea. I always thought, frankly, it was a point well taken.

But shall we get off the very boring subject of me? *I'm* not interesting. You can sum me up in about ten words: a former student of English literature who—who—who went downhill from there! Ha ha ha ha ha ha! Ha ha ha ha ha! Oh for God's sake.

For God's sake—no. Now, I'm serious—honestly—let's forget me and let's talk about someone who actually *is interesting*—let's talk about someone we can all *revere*!—now *that* would be enjoyable. In other words—yes—let's talk about—Howard!

But — er — ah — er-hrr — mm-hmm — er — now what can I say on such a fascinating subject? How should I begin to tell you about this remarkable man who responded so sensitively to the most obscure verses and also to the cries of the miserable and the downtrodden, sometimes virtually at the same instant, without ever leaving his breakfast table? I mean, if I'm going to speak of Howard, what should come first? What should be the very first thing that I ought to say? I mean, I really ought to say many *different* things *simultaneously*, because, you see, he was so outstanding in so many ways. But that's not possible. So what can I do? Oh what the hell—let's just calm down—I have to start *somewhere*—so—well—all right—I'll start by describing one of Howard's truly most exceptional qualities—well, let's just call it—his capacity for—for contempt. Yes.

Good. All right. So. "Howard's Capacity for Contempt." Now really, of course, that's really the subject for a lengthy monograph, I can only just sketch it, you know, a superficial sketch, but it really *is* a good place to begin, because Howard's capacity for contempt was so—well—incredibly vast. In fact, he really had contempt for pretty much everybody on earth. Isn't that absolutely wonderful?

HOWARD *(to Judy)*

All right, my darling. Hold my hand for a moment.

JACK

An apostle, you see, of universal love, but "flying through the day on wings of scorn," as some amusing wag said of someone once. Oh, it was impressive, really.

HOWARD *(to Judy and Jack)*

Oh God, I had to laugh when I heard what Tom was saying on the radio—ha ha ha—I really laughed.

JACK

It was wonderful, the way he could draw us all into it. Pretty soon we'd all be laughing.

(They all laugh.)

HOWARD

He was chattering, chattering, of course—to Eddie!—and all of a sudden—to Eddie's surprise —he was giving his famous views on "morality" again—aha ha ha!—

JACK

His contempt didn't come out of nowhere, of course. I mean, he had his reasons for being somewhat resentful. I mean, you had to understand that over the years—and a bit more each year, one could say, I suppose—poor Howard had really been frightfully mistreated in every possible way. Why, it was just outrageous! You know, a month after his very favorite little espresso bar in the park had been closed for good, they'd actually cut down his favorite grove of trees! And that's just one example. So naturally this was an angry man!

HOWARD *(to Judy and Jack)*

So immediately Eddie got very very serious. Oh yes, very serious—you know the way he gets. His lips get sort of—stuck in place—like this—you know? —so his voice is sort of "er er er"—hee hee hee—

(They all laugh.)

JACK *(to the audience)*

Now, one of *Judy*'s problems, I'm sorry to say, was that she refused to wear clothes in front of her father, which I, as her husband, found somehow always vaguely unnerving. I mean, her usual outfit around the house was this rather well-worn pair of ratty old trousers, some bright-red lipstick, and a rather frilly brassière. The trousers and lipstick never varied, but the brassière would be forgotten on certain occasions. In other words, she was sometimes topless. All right, all right, you think I'm a prude, but one of the main reasons it bothered me, honestly, was

that as Howard, of course, went around in his bed-
clothes and dressing gown, it meant that usually I
was the only one dressed. I mean, it was a little
unfair—don't you think so? I was the one who felt
out of place. I felt out of place because I was dressed!
Ha ha ha—

JUDY *(to the audience)*

Shall I tell you about the first time I met the very
amusing and extraordinarily long-lived President of
our country? I was about six years old, and I was
strolling happily through the park with my nurse,
running off the pathway every few moments to chase
a squirrel or a bird, and all of a sudden we passed
the President, also strolling, with a huge entourage.
He was heavily guarded in those days, obviously.
Well, as soon as we passed he ran back towards me,
with his whole group following confusedly behind
him, and he came right up to me, and he was sort
of pretending to be a cat, with his hands held up by
his ears like paws, and he was sort of purring and
miaowing, and then he laughed loudly and in-

structed me, "Now give your father my very best regards! Don't forget—my best regards!" And then he laughed again, and they were all gone.

So, who here can say what the difference is between poetry and prose? Can anyone tell me? Well—er—poetry comes in those short little lines! Isn't that the difference? Well, all right—all right, let's say it is. But can you tell me, then, how the length of the lines could possibly affect the way the words convey meaning? Do the words care what size of line they're on? But all the same, this indefinable difference has had some very definable results in *my* life over the years, in my opinion. You know, I always think of this drunken friend of Father's leaning over me sickeningly at some party or other when I was ten or eleven, saying, "Yes, it's a miracle, really, that he's allowed to exist, it's just remarkable that your father is allowed to exist!" Well, do you think he would have been "allowed to exist" past the age of thirty if he hadn't completely given up writing prose and devoted himself entirely to the writing of verse? It was just the way his talent developed, but it meant that the charming little gang who led our country never read what he wrote, as the only members of the gang who could understand poetry at all were undoubtedly Father's own father and our playful President himself, who, out of respect for his old comrade-in-arms, my appalling grandfather, undoubtedly made the decision just to look the other way.

JACK

Sometimes Howard would pick *me* to play the role of the idiot—Well, I guess he *always* did—ha ha ha—and that was really quite fun in a way.

HOWARD *(to Judy and Jack)*

Oh, I turned the volume on the radio to *loud*. I didn't want to miss a single word! Hee hee—did you know that morality was Eddie's favorite subject? Oh yes, he *loves* to talk about it. He finds it *so* enjoyable. You know, morality for Eddie is like—what?— like—what?—you know—it's like some terribly worthy old urn, some terribly worthy old urn that's wrapped up in some towels in his back closet. Well, it's got a few chips in it, one has to admit, and it is rather ugly, really, if you bother to look at it, and it's too heavy to lift, and in its style of course it's totally out of keeping with everything else in the house. So, well, you know, it can't be used, it has no function in his life at all—but ten times a day he has to exclaim, "Oh yes, that urn, it's my great possession, my greatest treasure."

JACK

But Howard, really, when you—

HOWARD

Now for Tom, of course, it's all just a wonderful way of being able to say at every opportunity, Well, I was superior. You know, Tom is really indifferent to other human beings. You could be dying in agony in front of his eyes, and it wouldn't bother Tom the slightest bit. But he loves morality because it means he can say, These other people were terrible, you know, what they did was wrong, they were inferior, contemptible. I, on the other hand, did what was right, you see, and I'm quite superior.

JUDY *(to the audience)*

His best piece of prose, I've always thought, was his essay called "The Enemy." You know, no one actually can write like that if they're over twenty-five, for whatever reason, and *he* most *certainly* never could have—it was all so bluntly personal: the way he wrote about his parents, the house, the corridors, the statues—the sheer lustfulness with which he described the young woman, whom he'd met in the park—the rather wild humor in his description of the process of bringing her over to the house . . . and then the power of that passage in which he slowly realizes who and what that young woman actually was. In the end, well, the hours he spent with her that night would change his life.

JACK *(to Howard)*

But really, Howard, after all—don't you think Tom *was* a bit superior? I mean, he did do some courageous things at certain crucial moments—you know, in comparison to someone like Martin—

HOWARD

Oh, really? In comparison to someone like Martin, do you think?

JACK *(to the audience)*

The best part was the way that once you were caught, and you couldn't move, he'd unsheath the knife and just slowly slide it into you.

HOWARD *(to Jack)*

But you see, there you're judging another human being. Aren't you? Jack? That's the thing that doesn't make sense to me. Because you're saying, in effect—you're saying, in effect, that Tom behaved the way he *should* have behaved, but Martin didn't. Martin ought to have behaved differently from the way he did behave. So you're implying—what?— that you think that you'd have behaved differently if *you* had been Martin?

JACK

I don't say *I* would have, but someone might have, yes.

HOWARD

But you see, that's where I become incredibly confused. Because I mean, if you were Martin, or if
someone were Martin, and they'd had Martin's life,
and Martin's experiences, then why wouldn't they
perceive the whole situation around them in exactly
the way that Martin did, and act accordingly? And
in that case, what's the point of condemning Martin?
Because he couldn't help being what he was—and
since he *was* what he was, he saw things the way
he saw them, and he did what he did.

JACK *(to the audience)*

And after the knife had gone in, he would just
continue.

HOWARD

I mean, you're putting your energy into praising
people or blaming people and saying who is better
and worse—and meanwhile your attention is entirely turned *away* from the human suffering that is
going on all around you and from the extremely
difficult, hard-to-answer question of what's bringing

it about. I mean, rather than condemning Martin or whomever, wouldn't it be more valuable to try to *understand* various things?—for example, to understand what circumstances in the world or in a person's life might lead them to behave the way Martin behaved? What are the circumstances which come up in the world and lead to that? And how do they come up? I mean, all the judging, all the condemning, who's superior, who's inferior, "I was right," and so on, are not terribly helpful to all the people who might actually be falling victim to every sort of horror while you're taking the time to debate these things.

JUDY *(to the audience)*

I've always loved the way he wrote in the essay about the people he called the "dirt-eaters," the people who eat dirt, and the ones, like this strange young woman, who rise up from the dirt to lead them. And in the final section, the way he described her as she sat there perched on his parents' sofa. Ten years later, you couldn't have found such a person anywhere, no matter how hard you looked.

J U D Y   A N D   H O W A R D *(reading out loud)*

"Drinking her tea from my grandmother's cup—yellow with flowers—"

H O W A R D *(reading)*

"—her hands nicked in a hundred places—she answered my questions politely, quietly. But even speaking softly, her voice was hard, like wire, wire twisting carefully around the simple words she spoke. How could someone like me even begin to imagine the life she lived? No safety. No hope. No shelter. No trees. A completely flat landscape going on forever. Running from the light, but the light was everywhere. When it rained, they were beaten into the ground, they had nowhere to go, lying in the mud. 'We've been wandering like this for, actually, years,' she said. Her beautiful skin, even her face —burned, scratched, like the fields she'd slept in."

J U D Y

For whatever reason—he was born that way—he had this odd ability—a quirky ability for someone from that background—he could read the face of anyone, effortlessly read it, and see the intelligence in it. So from an early age he was always wondering, Why were certain people—the ones *not* from his background—systematically made to eat dirt and kept so far away from the songs of Schubert?

HOWARD *(reading)*

"After she left, alone in my bedroom, lying on the floor, I frightened myself by how much I cried. So this was 'the enemy.' And all I wanted in the world was to help her. I said out loud, 'I'll do anything, anything.' But as soon as the words were out of my mouth, I was trembling with fear like the blind girl in the fairy tale."

JACK *(to the audience)*

People think I was fascinated by Howard's writing, that I'd always been some sort of admirer of Howard. That's simply absurd. You know, I was a confused young man. I was walking around some vaguely expensive clothing store one afternoon with a group of people. I was trying to buy a pair of pajamas. And along came Judy, also shopping, and

someone introduced us, and that thing happened—
you know, where people use that rather terrifying
expression, "Their eyes locked." And then Judy left,
but I kept having this really vivid fantasy that she
and I were both trying on pajamas, and I was taking
off my clothes and sort of wandering by mistake into
her little booth. And then a few weeks later I ran
into her again, late at night by the lake in the park
in that little alley of trees where they used to hang
those enormous paper lanterns. And eventually she
brought me over to the house, and I met Howard.
I met him, we talked, we got along fine. But my
God, I was never tempted for a single minute to
become a disciple of Howard. I was an observer, at
best. Even on a very good day, a *very* good day, a
vague hanger-on was the most I ever would have
called myself, if I would have called myself anything. That whole business of living at the whim of
another human being—watching out oh so carefully
for the moods, the sensitivities, on the great man's
face—well, that was terribly appealing to all those
delicate, melting, idealistic young girls who were

always hanging around, or the serious-faced young men in their dark overcoats, but God knows, not to me.

I mean, of course he was *remarkable*. Who would have denied it? It was remarkable simply to make all the *choices* he made: to dress in blues and greens, and not reds or grays; to know about the Sumerians, but not about the Assyrians. Sure, it was great. Although if you actually thought about it, it was all sort of arbitrary, really, in a way. Why blues, rather than reds, you see? I mean, there was no answer. I would say to myself every day, you know, Oh, he's accomplished so much, and I've accomplished nothing, so I really don't deserve to lick his boots. But I couldn't help it—it *did* bother me that all those wonderful choices that sort of made up the very fabric of Howard were, at their foundation, really sort of mindless.

But of course I envied him. What are you talking about? I envied the whole gang of them—all the old unbearables—Bob, Arthur, the whole crowd. And Howard? Come on. The possibility of not envying

Howard didn't even arise. It didn't even arise. Forget his writing—I envied him simply because of the way he could read. It was so easy, casual. The way I might have picked up an article about the latest approach to cooking string beans, he would pick up a book of poems by John Donne. I mean, I was clever enough to know that John Donne was offering something that was awfully enjoyable—I just wasn't clever enough to actually enjoy it. I'd devoted my life to it, I suppose you could say, but I couldn't get near to the great writers. Day after day and year after year, I read them and read them, but they always seemed remote. I didn't want them to. They just did. I was kept out of it all, kept away. Howard, on the other hand, was let right in. Come in, they said. Here we are. Come talk, come be with us. We're right here. Howard couldn't even comprehend what the problem was for the rest of us poor mortals. How could he, you see. But, do you know?— I always felt I was on the brink of understanding. I felt I could have learned. I was ready to learn. I would have humbled myself to any degree in order to learn, as a matter of fact. But he wouldn't teach me. None of them would. Howard, Judy, Bob, Arthur—the readers of poetry.

HOWARD

Jack wasn't actually a bad fellow, you know. I just found him a little bit vague at times. A little bit vague, a little bit lazy. You know, he *was* lazy. In fact, actually, he was so lazy that his favorite foods—I'm not making this up, because I observed it quite carefully—were soup, risotto, mashed potatoes, and ice cream. I'm not exaggerating!

JACK

God, I enjoyed watching Howard's reactions when Judy and I had just met, and I was just starting to come over to the house. You know, the thought of Judy and me being alone together was so horrifying to Howard that he would actually sort of follow us around, from room to room, without knowing he was doing it. I mean, for hours at a time he'd be creeping and crawling around us like some strange animal, his face frozen into this hideous little smile. At that time I happened to be living just a few streets away—I had a tiny apartment in one of those famous, awful cylindrical high-rises—and fairly often Judy and I would sort of spend the evening in my falling-apart bed with a bottle or two of something or other, and then we'd be hungry, and as I never had any food at my place, we'd get up, throw on a few clothes, and sneak very quietly into Howard's house to raid the refrigerator. Judy's face would be bright red, and she'd constantly be bursting out into that weird hysterical laugh she used to have then, and halfheartedly trying to muffle it, and when Howard would appear in his slippers with his special little smile, you could tell he found our whole manner just crassly, bluntly, appallingly obscene. Ha ha ha! Of course the comical part was that I happened to know, and Howard didn't, that I wasn't actually a good lover at all. God, no—I was really awful! Ha ha ha! I had no control over my own responses. I used to remind myself of my college friend Jorge who had this pet lemur which he kept on a leash and which was always leaping up at people unpredictably, or else lying down in some public place and refusing to budge, or starting to scream and refusing to stop, and I always used to think about Jorge's apologetic expression and gestures. In any case, women had always told me, you know, "You're not sensitive, you're very clumsy, the way you approach a woman's body is simply wrong." One woman had said, "You know, wrestling is really not the right model, try something else." But Judy knew absolutely nothing about sex, so she didn't mind. It all seemed great. Needless to say, I never pointed out to her, "Christ, you know, if you like me, you should try a man who can really do this." She was terribly happy. So we really spent years basically almost living there in Howard's house, and it wasn't that bad, but then things got so much better when we finally moved to our own little apartment—entirely on the other side of town from Howard! We moved in in April, and we had a little window, and from the tree outside these leaves grew into the window in the most voluptuous, irresistible, sexual way, and Judy and I grew sort of intertwined, getting up each morning with just the two of us—it was a wonderful time. Well, do I need to tell you it was a short interval? Good Lord—let's try to be realistic! Howard, after all, was in very poor health. I mean, he was much too sick, he was much too *ill*—he couldn't be expected to live by himself without Judy and me in the next room! And what possible value could our happiness have, in comparison to how seriously ill he was? He was *so ill*—the trouble was that no one could ever say in just what *way* he was ill, what was wrong with him exactly. He certainly had some awfully good days for someone who was so ill. For example, those who saw him on the day when he carried the logs from the garage to the house would probably be unlikely ever to forget it: up and down the driveway, up and down the driveway, sweat pouring off in sheets from his face, refusing rudely all offers of help, his eyes shining yellow like the eyes of a wolf . . . You see, during all those years, the only times I could really pull Judy totally away from Howard was when we'd go on a trip, when

we'd go to one of those awful places Judy loved—
one of the miserable places, tropical nightmare
zones—and those trips were so nice, really, because
no matter how sad or wistful Judy might have
seemed before we left—well, you know, introduce
her to a shepherd, or a couple of sheep, and she'd
perk right up.

JUDY

But the things that Father had said in his twenties
could not be unsaid. They didn't disappear. Their
consequences of course could be put off—sus-
pended—but not forever. Our beloved rulers were
naturally reluctant to show any unfriendliness to the
wayward son of one of their own, but that didn't
mean they didn't all read that little volume of essays
whose orange binding we knew so well, or that they
ever forgot it. No one did. Everyone knew that the
story wasn't over. And so people were often quite
nervous around Father. Some people were afraid to
meet him—you could see the tension filling their
faces—and there were others who saw him on a

daily basis, but the anxiety they felt somehow didn't diminish, or even increased. And of course I'm thinking of Joan more than anyone, really. You know, I always liked Joan the best of Father's friends—"The Rodent," as we called her, because she was thin and gray, or as Father once said, she was like a cloth you might use to polish silver with. I loved Joan, but she was a little weak. Loud and funny and wild when she played with us children —my friends always begged her to join our games —she was quiet with the grownups. Father meant everything to her—but one day she lost her nerve. I remember his face as he told me about it. "Joan's going away," he said. She went to live in a small suburb down by the water and never came back.

JACK *(to the audience)*

But almost as soon as we moved our belongings back to Howard's house—it was just at the beginning of the rainy season—things began to happen. And that whole awful year began to unfold.

HOWARD *(to Judy)*

Just help me, please, darling, come to me, please—

JUDY

What is it, Father?

HOWARD

What?

JUDY

Are you—what?—

HOWARD *(to the audience)*

Another wave of nausea washing over me, I'm praying for death, everything is dark, everything—sour. Terrible sounds. I need to talk to Judy—very important—

(to Judy)

What have you brought me?

JUDY

Bob left his book for you.

HOWARD

Extraordinary. Yes—this is magnificent—

(Weeping)

JUDY

Dad—

HOWARD

This is a drawing of a building which—

(Hearing something)

Did you hear something? God, what was that?—Is there any cereal?

JUDY

No, Dad.

(He continues weeping.)

JACK *(to the audience)*

First there was the rock through Howard's window. Who had thrown it? Did it mean something? Probably not, but you really couldn't tell. And then *my* thing started—you know, mental problems or whatever you'd call them. I don't even know how to tell the story or where I should begin it—I mean, mental phenomena—they're a little intangible—don't you think so? But anyway it happened that there was a certain moment one day, not long after the rock, when I just said to myself, Well, I'm going to spend a night away from this house, and so I packed a little suitcase, and I went and spent a night just all

by myself in a big hotel in a town about three hours
out on the railway line. Well, so, late that night, I
was lying in my tiny bed in my room in the hotel,
and I was reading a book of poetry by one of our
very finest authors, and all of a sudden I began to
hear sounds through the wall from the room next
door, and the couple next door began to tease each
other, they began to laugh, and while they laughed,
they started kissing, and they started moving around
in the room and falling into things. Well, suddenly
I was sitting straight up in my bed, and I knew I
had to decide very quickly, immediately in fact,
What should I do, what should I do, should I make
an effort to continue my reading, or instead should
I listen to the couple next door, maybe with one of
my hands sort of accidentally falling onto my dick?
There was no time to think—the couple next door
had stopped laughing now, they were groaning quietly with a sort of warm kind of gratitude—and so
I put the book down quietly on my bedside table.
And after the couple had finished making love—
and it took a long time—they went to bed, but I

couldn't sleep. My hand reached out toward the book on the table, but then I thought, Wait—do I really want to go back to reading that book? Might I not actually in fact prefer to read the magazine that I'd bought in the lobby, the one with all the stories about healthy, well-exercised, rather young actresses? So I read for a while in that very engaging magazine, but I still couldn't sleep, and so once again I started to reach for the book, but as I reached for the book my attention was drawn to the end of my bed, where a blank face looked expectantly into mine, a familiar framed screen which held inside it colors, songs, characters, drunkenness, love— beauty— And the faces that waited inside that blank face pulled me toward them, pulled my hand toward the knob to turn on the screen, and then toward my lamp to turn out the light. And as I sat in the darkness and watched the screen for hour after hour I thought to myelf, Well, at some point we have to draw some distinctions—don't we? I mean, pardon me, but shouldn't there be some distinction drawn between the things we say, the lies, the "I like poetry," "I like Rembrandt" on the one hand—and I mean, of course it's important to say those things, because after all if you don't say them then you really become simply a zoo animal, you become an empty *thing*, you're nothing more then really than a large balloon with a mouth, genitals, paws and an asshole, a nice great big one—but still they're lies, they *are* lies—and then on the other hand things that are true, like "I'm watching this very nice screen right now, I'm watching it, and I'm enjoying it"?

And so I came back to Howard's house, and days passed, and weeks passed, and I was sort of in a fog. I kept thinking nervously about all sorts of things. I was thinking a lot about the idea of the self. The self. The self. Or, as it's called from the inside, "I," you know—this strange little thing that everyone has, this odd, tiny organ which the surgeons can't touch. I remember being a boy and always reading these books which would refer excitedly to certain parts of the body as being "generously endowed with nerve endings," and now I wondered idly if the self was. On the whole, I thought not. It probably had no nerve endings at all.

Anyway, my mind was racing, speeding, in a peculiar condition, and one afternoon I found myself
pacing back and forth in Howard's living room, as
I often was on such afternoons, pacing and brooding, and I was sort of thinking about the fact that I
always walked around with this extremely stooped
posture, with my head sort of hanging down toward
the floor, and I suddenly asked myself, Why is that,
exactly? Could it possibly be because my head is too
heavy, because it's simply filled up with too much
stuff, with these rather large trunks, suitcases, and
worthless junk?

And then I asked myself, Well, what about that
noise I always hear, that intolerable noise which
comes from somewhere inside my head? And I realized consciously for the first time that, rather like
a singer who accompanies his own singing on the
piano or guitar, I accompanied my life with a sort
of endless inner tinkling, an endless noodling or
murmuring—a sort of awful inner murmuring of
reportage and opinions, idiotic arpeggios of self-
approbation—"Yes, this is what I'm doing, this is
what I'm doing, and this is the right thing to be

doing now, because murmur murmur murmur, and *this* is right because murmur murmur murmur, and *this* is right because murmur murmur murmur—" I thought about all the sincere consideration which I gave to the future, to my *plans*, you know, and all the solemn concern I lavished each day on the events of my past—my "memories," as we call them, wiping away a few tears—and I wondered: Was all this really tremendously valuable? Or was it perhaps just a bit unnecessary, when you consider the fact— rather often overlooked—that the past and the future don't actually exist? I sit around thinking about them from morning till night, but, you know, where *are* they? *Where are they?* I mean, they're not here. And God knows they're certainly not anywhere else, I would say. And so what is it supposed to *mean* to me if someone tells me that the trousers I'm wearing were worn "yesterday" by a man with my name, a man who did this, a man who did that, or that they'll be worn "tomorrow" by a man who is going to be doing something or other? It all means exactly *nothing* to me, because none of these people actually exist.

JUDY

Suddenly, there were a group of rather quiet demonstrations on some rather quiet streets, leading
people to ask, Well, were these demonstrations the
usual fakes—or were they, could they be, real this
time? Could we possibly be seeing the awakening
of "the enemy" after all these years? Were "the dirt-
eaters" somehow gently stirring? And were certain
people whose hands were nicked in a hundred
places suddenly making their presence felt? That
would be funny, after we'd been told for so long that
people of that sort no longer existed. And then, perhaps as a consequence of these developments, or
maybe not—well, to use that perennially popular
metaphor from cards—there were cabinet shuffles,
over and over. And every time that the big govern-
mental deck would be cut, more people we'd never
heard of would rise to the top of it. Was it a card
game or a card *trick*? The old officeholders, the filthy
herd of swine whom we vaguely knew and would
even vaguely nod to at cocktail parties, were quietly
replaced by a new herd of swine whom we *didn't*
know—the new generation, who dressed in new

colors—those chalky colors, yellow and pink and various greens—and lived in new neighborhoods, and even ate in new restaurants with new styles of cooking.

JACK

When I was growing up, there was an uncle of mine who always used to tell me, "Look, we are rats. All of our family have always been rats, and you, too, will be a rat, my boy. Remember that, and you won't go wrong, because it's really all quite simple: The skills rats possess don't work under water, so avoid getting wet. Don't abandon the sinking ship unless another boat's nearby to board. And, for God's sake, don't be ashamed of being a rat. Rats aren't bad, they're not mean or cruel, they're simply doing what they can to survive." Well, the point is that Howard, you see, in contrast to my uncle, was a rather contrary son of a bitch. He too was born unmistakably a rat—I mean, there are signs at birth—the predatory placement of the nostrils, you know, indicating that the creature so marked intends to grow up to be sleek, fat, and healthy and will do what it needs to do throughout its life to *stay* sleek, fat, and healthy, which is the beautifully invariable destiny of the rat. Alertness, in other words, self-protection, self-defense, and the ability if necessary to preemptively attack. But you see, Howard was born a rat, but he sort of declined to be one. He "simply refused." The petulant, pouting, preening old twit. Well, you have to admire him for it in a way, I suppose. But the point is that he passionately believed that the worst thing in the world that a person could be was, actually, a rat. To be a rat was just unutterably vile. And I of course knew that in fact I was one. When I looked in the mirror I saw a rat. Well, for that matter, when I looked at *him* I saw a rat, but that was something that no one was supposed to point out, or no one was *allowed* to point out. His wife was polite and had shut up about it. In fact some people said she was so polite that she'd literally died rather than mention it. But in any case the strange fact was that Judy and Arthur and Bob and that whole crowd of people believed themselves to be tiny, beleaguered, innocent creatures living in a world of rats, dominated by a government which was run by rats, where the crude, survival-driven taste of rats was everywhere triumphant and growing more powerful every day, and far from wondering whether Howard was a rat, they actually begged him to be their great leader in the war *against* the rats, the war against everything for which they held the rats responsible, from the unattractive figurines in the sculpture garden to the lamentable fact that there were no more free concerts—and for about fifteen minutes I was invited to be a sort of foot soldier myself in the war against the rats, if you want to see it that way. Never, mind you—sniff— asked to join the ranks of the *officers'* corps—boo- hoo boo-hoo—not quite the right *material*, I'm sure you understand—now isn't that sad?—his own son- in-law?—but perhaps almost worthy to be a low- grade sort of cheerful cannon fodder—aha ha ha—

But anyway, all this talk about war and soldiers brings me to the much-discussed question of "ene- mies," you see, and that's a question that we really have to face. I mean, when people refer to quote unquote "the enemy," "our enemies," they're referring, basically, to what someone once called "the snarling, snapping, unmuzzled dogs"—I love that phrase—"the snarling, snapping, unmuzzled dogs"—ha ha ha—in other words, the individuals who live, so to speak, "outside the fence," quote unquote, the ones who are camped on the other side of the fence with their campfires, their pots, their marshmallows or whatever the hell they have over there.

In other words, you see, if you look at the world, the world as a whole, actually most people in it are the ones we can only refer to, rather nervously and gingerly, by means of those terribly melodramatic and almost hysterical words like "wretched," "miserable," "unfortunate," "desperate," "powerless," "poor"—that's a very sympathetic one—or to put it a bit differently, God bless them, they're people who simply don't have any resources of any kind at all. And these particular people—and, you know, God knows why—well, they just don't like us. They *don't like us.* They simply don't like us. So it's not hard to see what will happen one day. There's the majority, them, the minority, us, and the way they feel about us, great dislike, very very great dislike. So, in other words, "enemies" are not exactly imaginary beings. They're very, very real. But I'll tell you something interesting about enemies, you see. At least this is how I feel about it. I'm sure you know that rather nasty and not terribly thought-provoking old saying that "the enemy of my enemies is my friend." Well, what's really much more true to *my* sense of life is that the friend of my enemies is for sure my enemy, while in a funny way my enemies themselves don't bother me that much, and in an odd way I can even work up quite a bit of respect for them, looking at it all from a certain point of view.

It's that thing of people whom you actually know and with whom you actually live *deciding consciously* to be the friend of your enemies that can get you really terribly upset, because your enemies after all are actually trying very hard to kill you, no matter what you may happen to feel about them—and this

is where things with Judy and Howard really became so difficult, because they'd worked themselves
around to being so horribly appalled by the revolting
rats that they saw encroaching everywhere on their
perfect existence that they ultimately decided that
the people whom they actually ought to *like* were,
yes, that's right, precisely the ones who were sitting
around making plans to slice our guts out, or in
other words to perform that gesture cleverly referred
to by one of our enemy-loving writers as "the dis-
emboweling of the overboweled." And that became
ultimately rather revolting to me.

Weirdly, I suppose—and who can really say for
sure about this kind of thing?—you might say that
the beginning of the beginning of the end for me
with dear old Howard came about one night when
we were all sitting around after an early dinner—
Howard, Judy, and the usual crowd—and suddenly
everyone decided we should go to see a play, we
should all go off to see this play that had been incredibly popular for that whole year, *The Trojan
Horse* by Reginald Longleat. I suppose maybe they

were all in one of their occasional fits of sociological prurience and just wanted to see what nonsense the public was consuming that year or God knows what. I imagine I went along because maybe I actually thought I would like the play, have some fun, even enjoy myself, God forbid, or some such absurdity. Anyway, I guess I must have been the last one in line to buy my ticket to the play, because the others were sitting all together in a group, and I sat alone two rows in front of them.

Well, the play was supposed to be this charming comedy, but the writer's hatred for the human race—or for everyone not just exactly like him, one might say—kept oozing out of it, like blood oozing out from a closet full of bodies. There was something about the writing—it was horribly jarring. One was constantly wondering, how in the world had he chosen these particular words? Was he just simply out of his mind, or what? Can any word at all be used? In any way? Longleat's approach to grammatical forms made me think of some sort of corrupt plumber who had screwed into alignment some series of pipes that never were intended to fit together—where, I mean, the whole thing was absolutely bound to explode, but maybe not until its maker was safely out of town. It was all so ugly, and the whole play was incredibly boring, and it wasn't even funny, because all of the jokes fell totally flat. You know, and as I sat there watching this awful play, I began to feel a rather unexpected longing to turn around in my seat and look back at Howard. I mean, this happened to be one odd moment when I really wanted to see Howard's face. I wanted to see that look of incredulous dismay, that rather exaggerated expression which even from a very great distance away you could read as saying, "Good God, is this actually occurring?" So when Longleat served up this particularly witless, terrible joke—it was vicious as well, if one happened to think about it, and the sadistic audience was hooting with pleasure—I twisted around quite suddenly in my seat and looked directly over at our little group, but none of them saw me. They were laughing their heads off, Howard even more than the others. He was roaring with laughter, in that eloquent phrase, and for a moment everything stopped, and I felt a very quiet but forceful spinning sensation.

Well, so the next week was my birthday, and Judy had decided to have a party for me: about fifty people, all of their friends and even people *I* liked—a regular party—paper hats, toy trumpets, games on the lawn. Croquet, et cetera. And Howard had said, I'll barbecue the meat. So it was the day of the party, and people began to come over around five, and one of the families brought along a girl who was a student from Denmark. Well, I was drinking and joking around, and for whatever reason—and I wouldn't know, because I'm not at all familiar with Danish culture—this student was quite attracted to me and found me very amusing and kept brushing up against me. So somehow we both wandered off into the garage, and without giving the whole thing a great deal of thought we were somehow kissing, and I'd put my hand underneath her shirt and was fondling her breasts. Well, all of a sudden Howard walked into the garage—to get some coal for the

barbecue, I suppose—and it was this farcical moment. The Danish girl ran into the house, Howard
ran off in the direction of the lawn, and I really didn't
know quite where to go, so I went into the tool shed.
Well, there was nothing really to do in the tool shed,
so I sat there simply playing with my dick. And while
I was playing with my dick, I looked through a little
eye-level window, and I saw Howard wandering
around on the lawn, not quite sure just how he
should proceed, and I thought to myself, I can't
stand this man, I can't stand this man, and I don't
believe anything this man believes. Not a single
thing.

JUDY

God, you know, it was so fitting in a way—everything started when I was at a concert! Emotional
works for string orchestra. I'd decided to go off to
spend an evening by myself, and I sat there watching, blissfully watching, watching the musicians under the bright lights. They were playing wonderfully,
leaning forward, so committed, their heels digging

into the stage—and then suddenly the lights seemed to flicker for a moment, but the players went on playing—and then all at once we were in total darkness. The audience made an odd little sound, like the hoarse sound of a broken bell, and started to run. I thought of a movie I'd seen of cows in a corral. Then a door opened at the back of the stage, and we could see through it into the street. Behind the scurrying musicians holding their instruments to their chests we saw flashes of light, and then— impossible—then we heard shots—not one or two pops, but shooting like you'd hear on the evening news, a sound that in spite of everything we never really thought we'd hear "live," so to speak. And so that was it. Everything started over from that moment.

A few days—a month—and all of a sudden ten thousand examples of "human remains," as the newspapers called them—"human remains"—or was it fifteen thousand?—had shown up in every sort of inappropriate spot, such as the carousel in the middle of the park, and at least that many people had been unceremoniously arrested by the police. There was a week when we went to three funerals of friends. Two had been sitting quietly in restaurants. Someone had come in, had said, "Don't get up," then walked behind them and shot a hole in the back of their heads, blood pouring out of them onto their plates.

Well—it hadn't happened for a long time, but now it was happening once again. Those who were suffering had whimpered a little, they'd made themselves known, and so of course it was inevitable that the serious individuals who led our country would begin to respond. As in all such periods, you could never predict the form of the response, just its filthiness.

Naturally the economy flew out of control. No more pet food. We gave all our animals to friends who had farms, except that I insisted on keeping the cat.

Jack wanted me to leave, to go live with him and let poor Father take care of himself. He kept saying, for some reason, that Father was not some special human being—Father was no different from anyone else. Father enjoyed wearing nice-looking shirts, so in Jack's view he was no different from someone like Martin, who happened to wear the same type of shirts—never mind that Martin would happily have slit his grandmother's throat to get the money to *buy* them. And Jack never stopped trying to get me to agree that Father's taste in music was actually quite vulgar. Well, maybe it was, but I didn't really see what Jack was trying to prove.

JACK

From then on, more and more often I'd find my mind had just slipped away from me, following some peculiar will of its own. One day she said to me something like, "I don't understand your relationship to society. I don't understand your relationship to the world you live in." "Can I tell you something?" I said to her snappily. "Do you know something? I don't understand my relationship to my own *ass*. I mean, I was standing naked in the bathroom this morning, and when I saw my ass in the mirror I just said to myself, "What *is* that? What *is* that?

And what does it have to do with me?" The strange
thing was that I was talking so much and saying
things—

JUDY

Jack—

JACK

Yes?

JUDY

Jack—

JACK

What? Jesus Christ, will you stop bothering me?

(to the audience)

but I could perfectly well have said other things
instead.

JUDY

Jack—*people cry at funerals.*

JACK

Excuse me?

JUDY

People cry at funerals.

JACK

I know that, Judy. I know that, you see. You stupid
bitch. Look, I've tried to tell you about myself, about

what I'm like, over the years, but your mind, apparently, has always been somewhere else, unfortunately. And now what are you saying? That I've let you down? I'm a disappointment? I paid you the respect of trying to tell you the fucking truth. And now you're blaming *me* because *you* didn't pay any fucking attention? You cold, unfeeling, inhuman bitch.

JUDY *(to the audience)*

"Can't I be saved?" I cried out to him, falling on my face in the grass, hugging his legs. "No," he said. "Love can't save you." "But what about the idea of a better world?" I said.

JACK

I did take a bath this morning, if that's what you're asking. What are you asking?

JUDY

I'm asking you, Don't you—don't you—don't you remember how you felt when we went to visit that fucking *orphanage*?

JACK

Where was that, actually?

JUDY

—with the orange trees outside it? We *saw* the children, we *touched* them—your shirt was soaked with the sweat of that sick little girl—I mean, what *are* you now? Do you see yourself now as just—what? As what?

JACK

I don't see myself "as" anything at all. Judy, you see, you're looking at me. This is me. This is me, and this is all there is to me.

JUDY

Jack—please—

JACK

Tell me what you're telling me.

JUDY

The orphanage—the infirmary—the orange trees— the girl—the medicine—the beds—

JACK

Spare me all the talk, Judy. I'm not interested in talk. Do you see what I'm saying? If you love me, well, make a sacrifice for me. Take a risk for me. Suffer for me. Otherwise, what are you talking *about*? You're talking about nothing. I don't have time for it, I have no interest in it, it's worth nothing to me.

JUDY (to the audience)

I said to him, Yes, you can't imagine it, but yes— the many living under the heel of the few—one day it *will* end. I believe it will end. For you, that's a joke. You can't picture it. But I can.

JACK (to Judy)

Judy, I don't know what to say. I mean, for God's sake, what's happening? I kiss you, and it's as if my kiss goes hurtling off a cliff. You take off your clothes, but you're not naked. What can we do, then? What will happen?

(to the audience)

"You made me," she said, trying to sum up all the things that had happened over years. "You made me. And then you annihilated me. And then you breathed on the corpse and awakened me. Over and over. How could a life like that have gone on forever?"

Useless to hold her hand, to try to explain. Here's

my explanation: I felt this, I felt that. No. That's not an explanation. You know what love is, you know what grief is.

JUDY *(to the audience)*

A group of men on the front lawn—they asked to see Father. They looked like the people who came over all the time. Father put a robe on over his pajamas, put on his slippers, came downstairs. They said nothing, they smashed his face in with their hands and fists, left him bleeding, and ran away.

The next day Jack moved out of the house.

JACK *(to the audience)*

Oh, I don't know. It was a day when finally something just broke in my head, and I was in terrible shape. Then I ran out of the house, and I felt better, so I never went back. You know, it was actually my body that ran out of the house—do you see what I'm saying? What propelled it, it didn't know, and no one knows. No one can know, and no one will ever know. I can certainly describe the afternoon. It was very cold. It was a horrible, horrible cold afternoon, and I was freezing cold. For a long time I was trudging back and forth down the gloomy hallway of the upper story of Howard's house, and of course there'd been the beating up of Howard just the day before, and so every few minutes I'd hear a painful sound coming out of the room where he lay, where he lay coughing and choking in a mess of bandages. Christ, what could be done for poor Howard? He was all alone. A tiny little man, like a little fly, in that big bed. No one to help him.

Then eventually I entered our own bedroom, and there was Judy, wrapped up in our bed. She too wasn't well, or you could say she was exhausted, hadn't slept, whatever, and she too was freezing cold, she immediately informed me. I sat right down in a chair by the bed and looked at her face for a long time. Well, I mean—you know, I guess we were talking, in a manner of speaking. And at a certain moment I felt I saw her skin grow suddenly pale, and I thought, Oh yes, the pallor of a corpse. It's quite clear, isn't it? Her tongue, as she spoke, was like a child's lollipop. And then for some reason she stopped speaking. Pulling the sleeves of her sweater out over her hands to keep in the warmth, her teeth chattering. So we sat there silently, neither of us able to move at all. I quite honestly didn't have much that I wanted to say. I knew what she would say, I knew what I would say—so why say it? It was really as if she was tied to the bed, and as I sat beside her, a heavy silence kept hitting us repeatedly, like a wet towel, repeatedly hitting, till our faces were red, sore, wet, then bloody. Make love to her, I thought—or murder her, maybe. Maybe that was really the thing, after all. Well, she knew what I was thinking before I thought it, and she was sick with fear. Literally sick. With fear of me. And I thought of all those years of getting up every day and reading in the newspaper all those terrible stories, always written in that special tone, so hurt, so shocked, about the people who committed unspeakable acts. The murder. The stabbing. "How could anyone commit such an unspeakable act?" It was all falling away, falling away very fast. How much longer could

I keep on pretending to be hurt and shocked by unspeakable acts?

Now she seemed to be falling asleep, and I thought I saw a corpse with a beaten-in face. The rain poured down as I hurried into the garden. A shovel, the gardening shears—anything, anything. She was waiting for me—no time to spare. On the lawn I tripped on a croquet mallet. That would do.

Something had simply ended, that was all. As if all those years had been just a moment. She'd stretched her hand into the water to save me from drowning. I had felt that beautiful, long bony hand catch on to my hand and hold on tight. But I was much too heavy, moving too fast—I'd fallen out and gone down.

I came back from the garden and looked in the bedroom. Something was wrong—something was wrong with my baby. Her sleep was troubled—she was shuddering and snuffling.

I put the mallet down gently against the wall, and then I stood by the bed and watched her as she slept for a very long time. How could so much joy, so much happiness for me, have been contained in this one little package?

Well, can't there be a silent language? Must we talk? I felt I was falling through a spiraling darkness, blackness filling my lungs. I got into the bed. I could hear her voice.

JUDY

Let's go quietly.

JACK

Then when I woke up, my face felt wet. Tears? No—it seemed to be blood. The cat had clawed me. A few whiskers had been left on the pillow as a sign.

Then I wondered, Why weren't the lights out, if I'd been sleeping?

Regrettably, the cat had not been recently fed, I recalled. I tried to remember quickly what was happening in my life. There was a reason, obviously, for the cat's condition. And yes, I myself was also hungry. Why? What had happened?

JUDY

Let's go quietly.

JACK

When I woke up this time, there was a sound of rockets. Shells, a battlefield. I'm badly wounded, and they're carrying me along by a river of blood. I'm trying to spit out my own teeth.

Then, inside the hospital, everyone's kind, polite. I'm lifted onto a clean bed. My bowels wiped up. I'm washed, bandaged. Someone brings some food on a tray, and with all my strength I swing my arm and send the food flying all over the room.

Then a long night follows. A nurse sits near me. At one moment I wake up, and I see her smiling. She looks right in my eyes and draws a finger across her throat.

JUDY AND HOWARD

Let's go quietly.

JUDY

You remember the place. Past the bell tower, the
meadow—

JUDY AND HOWARD

Let's go quietly.

JUDY

—the trees, the clearing—

JUDY AND HOWARD

Let's go quietly.

JUDY

—the metal sculpture—you said "a swan or a
duck"—

JUDY AND HOWARD

Let's—go—

JUDY

—the track where the children ride in carts—

JUDY AND HOWARD

—quietly.

JUDY

And please, darling, would you just be very simple at the end of your life? Could you tell me you
"love" me? Say, "I love you," use those very words?—

those very same words that have been used by everyone—by the poor, the ugly, the stupid, the weak?

And you know, the silly thing is that I still can't think of the name of that actress—I mean, the one who played the sister of Tarzan's wife. But do you remember that movie where she played a nurse? My favorite part was that incredible scene where she's lying in bed with this frightening guy, and all of a sudden there's this amazing, wonderful shot of her ass—just this absolutely gorgeous, beautiful ass, seen from above—and you hear her dialogue while you look at her ass, and it's as if the dialogue were somehow literally being spoken by her ass, and it's so incredible.

JACK *(to Judy)*

For God's sake, don't you have any feelings at all? For the sake of Jesus—you're trying to kill me!

(to the audience)

I was awakened by the sound of my own shouting. I ran out of the house, and I was out for good.

HOWARD

There was a fantasy I always used to have about Joan. Maybe I dreamt it too. I'm lying in bed with warm pillows and blankets, and there's a low fire sitting in the grate, and Joan comes into the room with a delicious sandwich on a white dish. And after I've eaten it, she sits beside me and we look out the window as she holds me very tightly.

Through the window, under a bright moon, we see horses playing on the grass, and birds playing in the sky above the house. And her very cold hand is stroking me slowly but purposefully with a delicate motion, up and down, and I'm thinking about this whole rather twisted question of death, and I say to myself, For God's sake, will you stop struggling? Lie back. Put your head on the pillow. Close your eyes. Don't you know how to enjoy *anything*? Just wait for the moment which you know will come. There. There. One, two—it's a certainty.

PART TWO

JUDY *(to the audience)*

Then one day there was a funny postcard with a picture of an outdoor restaurant—no salutation, no signature. *(She reads.)* "In a very pretty garden, I ate lunch without you today. At a wobbly table with a thin rose crawling bent and unbalanced out of a tiny vase, I ate an egg and didn't think about you."

JACK *(to the audience)*

I stayed in a little hotel for a while. An adorable hotel—fruit, a few plants, whitewashed walls, and that was about it. Except I kept having—guess what—memories. Not particularly painful memories, but one day I found myself brooding about an article I'd seen that had some interesting pictures that had accompanied it: I was thinking particularly of two specific pictures of the very nice, charming, good-natured actor who was the subject of the article, and one of them showed him kissing his wife, and then the other one showed him when he was acting in a movie, and he was kissing the woman who played his wife in the movie, and he looked exactly the same in both pictures, and at the time I'd read the article I'd said to myself, He's a liar, he's lying, he's lying in one of these pictures at least. But now as I thought about it, I suddenly thought, Wait a minute, no, he's *not* lying. He's *not* lying. He's *not* lying, because he's not pretending to be the same person in both pictures. Jesus Christ—that *actor* wasn't lying, *I'm* the one who's lying when I keep on insisting that I *am* the same person—the same person I was this morning, the same person I was yesterday. What's *that* all about? And why do I do it? What is the point? Why am I struggling every day to learn my lines, to once again impersonate this awful character—this terrible character whom I somehow believe I've been chosen to play, this terrible character whose particular characteristics are impossible to remember? I feel exactly the way a criminal must feel, trying so hard every day to stick to the story he was telling yesterday, the alibis, the lies, the interconnected details—it can't be done, you can't remember it all. So why do I keep trying to pretend to be the same, when in fact my body is simply a shell, waiting to be filled by one person and then another?

After I'd stayed in the hotel for several weeks, I developed the habit of walking in the park, and one day in the middle of the park I was standing at a lemonade stand drinking lemonade, and I happened to meet a very sweet girl. She was with some friends, but she was standing apart from them, and, I don't know why, I felt I'd feel comfortable talking to her, so I just started talking, and she responded in a quiet little voice. Her little pink mouth was so small, it was just like a little tiny mouse mouth really, her little skirt like a bit of foam from the sea, her shoes like miniature containers for sewing equipment. We talked for a while, and her friends then said they were going to leave, but she stayed behind, and we kept on talking. In that quiet little voice she told me about a sensation she said she'd been experiencing lately—"almost as if I'm in a picture," she said, "and something smudged it." "Is there also almost like a sort of funny silence?" I asked. "Yes. I think so—" "Well, don't you know what that is?" I said with a laugh. "I think that's despair . . . aha ha ha—"

I went out for a while with the lemonade-stand girl. I had an affair with her, you see. Shall I tell you the subtle approach I used to lure her into it? Well, we were standing there at the lemonade stand, and it was getting dark, and I looked her in the eye, and I said to her, "Would you like to have an affair with me?" Wasn't that clever? She responded by touching me a little bit crudely. Then she introduced herself—her name was Peg—and we went to her apartment.

I often cried in bed when Peg and I made love, because I felt like a lamb who was feeding on grass, and folk tales tell us that happy lambs quite often cry.

Holding me in her arms, Peg was limitlessly kind. Her goodness was sort of like an ocean, really, and

I was free to swim in it, and I swam and felt free.

You know, I'd always wondered, How can people say that they're moved by nature—how could that be possible, when the tree, the flower, have really no meaning? No one made them, no one intended anything particular by them, so how can people say that they mean something, is that not like the belief of someone insane who thinks the raindrops on the window are bringing him a message? No—not at all—lying next to Peg, I saw I'd been wrong. It was easy now just to look at her shoulder, her neck, her cheek, and receive a kind of direct communication, as if her body were literally speaking to mine, as if I was able to hear things now, a stone talking, or a tree stump at night, or the moon.

Anyway, things didn't work out with Peg. She got tired of me. Maybe my problem was just having always been very unhappy—you know, unhappiness being a kind of cold sort of marshland in which other emotions just refuse to grow.

One day, lying on a beach after swimming, our teeth chattering, her goose-bumped skin pressed close against mine, she said, "Jack, I love you," and I thought: What does she mean? Is she talking about me? My name rang so oddly in my ears.

JUDY

Each night, alone in the house with Father, I'd go to bed late. I'd fall asleep instantly, as if I'd been clubbed, then three hours later I'd wake up again —sweaty, terrified, my heart pounding. Lying in my bathtub in the dark, I'd twist back and forth under the little stream of water as if an invisible person were whipping me brutally. Mustn't touch myself, I'd think. That would be bad. The wrong direction.

All Father's friends were putting pressure on me, as if I were the one who had all the answers, somehow, as if I could explain what was going on. Why? Why me? I'd wait and wait, then dawn would come, and the distant sound of violence—that vague, low roaring and groaning, the snapping of guns—would finally grow quiet, or almost quiet. That heartsick feeling didn't go away, the oppression, the awfulness—but yes, sure, it was soothing, it was comforting, to feel the sweetness of the morning air, to hear the birds, the insects.

Every once in a while I'd still sometimes throw on some earrings and a dress and go to a party at some embassy or other and chat with the bureaucrats, the wives, the rising young couples. But I learned nothing, really nothing, beyond the obvious fact that half the high officials were in their twenties now.

JACK

After a while I just concluded there wasn't any hope—an important insight. There'd be no happiness in my own life, nor would peace be won in the world at large. Was there anything, then, that I could expect to achieve in the coming years? Well, perhaps I could somehow train my mind to focus less compulsively on terrifying images of death and disease. Perhaps I could learn how to pass more easily from one moment to the next, the way the monkey, our ancestor, shifts so easily along from branch to branch as he follows the high road through the forest at night. Let me learn how to repose in the quiet shade of a nice square of chocolate, a nice slice of cake. A delicious cup of tea isn't, perhaps, that hard to come by; the trick to be learned is just not to think of other things while you drink it.

JUDY

The radio broadcast some absurd message. There were to be some new people in high positions, some new policies, all very vague, but from the tone of it you knew it was going to be bad. Everyone was talking on the telephone all day, and most of the old friends—the ones who were left—wanted to come over to the house—we knew we wanted to be together. Father got inspired and decided to cook.

And so that afternoon around five they all came, shambling through the courtyard into the garden to stand once again under the stiff little trees with their frozen pods. The sky was gray, the breeze was icy. Mary was there, and Herbert, and Arthur, and Bob, and Sam. Sam brought a jar of Indian chutney, which made a nice complement to Father's meat.

As dusk fell in the garden, we could hear these really extraordinary sounds—you know, the boom of explosions, and very loud shots. We knew they were nearer than they'd ever been before. Still we sat at the garden table or strolled near it, eating the meal Father had prepared. The odor of the flowers seemed peculiarly strong, as if their last drops of perfume were being squeezed into the air in the knowledge that no one would be able to smell them later. No one ate much, but we all ate something.

Finally, as the sounds of shooting got louder, we all drifted inside—it was pure mindless instinct. A light, almost invisible drizzle had begun, so we pretended to ourselves that we simply were going inside to keep dry. There were ominous silent flashes—a bluish tint to the air. And the dusk deepened.

Inside, we stood in the kitchen, moving unnaturally slowly and quietly, no one standing too close to anyone else. "Listen," Bob said. We all listened; and we heard birds approaching. Flapping, flapping—an almost equestrian sound—sort of like the proverbial "thunder of hooves." "Well," Father said, "I'm not exactly known as a superstitious man"—and the flapping got a notch louder—"but the appearance at such a moment of such an enormous cloud of birds . . ."

We turned toward him abruptly, because when he spoke his voice had taken on a peculiar timbre —something like that rich, honeyed sound it had had once when he'd caught pneumonia years ago.

And then no one spoke for a long time—each one just shifting his weight from foot to foot in his own little circle. I suddenly felt a terrible cramp in my stomach, and I bent over. And then I opened my mouth, and light seemed to pour out of it onto the ground. I could feel, as if it were happening to me, the penis of every man in the room slowly starting to rise. I was crouched over, close to the floor, surrounded by a forest of men, each with a branch at the groin sticking sharply up.

And then, with a crack, the rain was suddenly beating down on the garden, rattling wildly on the windows. And after a little time, through the roar of the rain, I heard the sound of breaking glass, as if bottles were being thrown and broken. And then the grinding gears of a truck pulling up, stopping in the driveway just where the milkman's truck always used to stop. Would they ring the bell like the milkman used to do, to give us the bill?

We drifted into the living room. Arthur sat in a chair—so did Bob, Mary—and their bodies slowly sort of curled up in the chairs. Their expressions, really, were just of waiting, a little bit puzzled, like patients sitting in their pajamas in hospitals. Then there were sounds of commotion in the garden, and at first no one even went to the window to find out what was happening. I finally did, though, and in the darkness and rain the light from the house picked out a few spots I could see on the lawn. A patch of flowers. Some dishes, food. I saw a blur of men moving quickly around. Then, by the table where we'd all had our meal, I saw a dead person lying—an old man—his skull had been crushed. He lay in the mud, face downward, the rain pouring over him, the inside of his head washing out onto the lawn.

As a child I'd always read about "biting down on cyanide capsules"—I'd imagined the faint taste of the gelatin of the capsules—or the frightening, painful bits of glass if the capsules were of glass. And I actually wondered, as all this happened, if such things as cyanide capsules existed anymore.

I thought of the weight, the heaviness of Jack as he lay on top of me. And then—it was almost funny, simply because it was so exactly like what one had always imagined—they knocked on the door.

So yes, we landed exactly where we knew we would land, like parachutists. Like the last pieces of a puzzle, we floated down into the space that had been waiting. And once it was happening, it seemed right, and all the times we'd prayed, God, don't let it happen, seemed far away.

I excused myself, went upstairs to the toilet, and vomited. Then I brushed my teeth, went back downstairs, and I was more or less fine. Shivering a bit as we went out into the rain, but still perfectly able to walk to the truck.

God, I'd spent a lifetime being afraid of being

locked in a cell, of being slapped in the face, of being punched, of being watched by someone while I sat on the toilet—in one second, it all dropped away. I let go of it in a second. Like opening a fist. Letting a bird out of a cage. Not the sound of a door closing—it felt like the sound of a door opening: a girl whom someone has locked in her room; then the sound of her footsteps clattering as she bursts out, then runs outside.

JACK

Judy and Howard and their friends went to prison. Ha ha ha—it seems fantastic to say that—I never thought I'd be saying that sentence about people I knew—"They went to prison"—ha ha ha. And it was a hard time, and a long time—five years. Arthur and Bob—well, they died fairly soon. You know, if there was a draft coming through a window in a restaurant, it was too much for Arthur, so I suppose you can imagine that the famously cold, famously damp climate of our rather famous local prison didn't agree with him at all, or with Bob either. They shriveled up like little mice and died. Mary, a bit hardier, lived three years, and Herbert four. Then, finally, Sam died, and—well—by the end of the five years, only two of the old gang were there to be released—Judy, by decades the youngest, and—can it be true?—guess quick before I say—yes—in fact—the other was—that terribly delicate, terribly infirm old man—Howard! Ha ha ha— Oh God, what a surprise! Strangely, of course, by the time they came out, although Howard naturally found himself in the best of health, Judy was sick with something or other—one of those illnesses that keeps going away and then coming back.

One night when Judy and Howard were in prison, I was at a party, sort of stuffing myself with cheese-cake and pie, and I started talking with this rather eccentric, rather dizzy older woman. I guess she was drunk. I know I was. She looked like she didn't go to parties all that often, and the outfit she wore was somewhat bizarre. All of a sudden I had a blinding intuition. "Wait—you're Joan!" I suddenly said, and I was absolutely right. Isn't that amazing? It was the legendary Joan. And because we were drunk we had a long, frank talk, and at one point she said, "Well, what was your problem with Howard, basically?" "Oh I don't know," I said. "I guess it was how much I hated him, really." "Yes, exactly, that was my problem too," she heartily agreed.

To be quite frank, one has to say those were not bad years for a lot of people. A lot of people were getting by, not doing that badly, or even doing a bit better than that. I myself had a pretty good job. I wrote a column on sex for *The Morning Urinal*, as everyone absolutely insisted on calling it. It wasn't really such a terrible paper, but everyone just loved to make fun of it, for some reason—it showed people's boldly independent spirits, I suppose.

After all he'd gone through, poor Howard didn't get to celebrate much after he got out of prison. Actually, it might seem to be, you know, a little absurd to lock somebody up for five years and *then* have someone come to his house and shoot him—all basically because of a couple of essays he'd written several decades before—but you have to understand that no one person plans these things: person A decides the first thing, person B decides the second, you know, I mean, that's just how it works.

Someone had a fetish about mealtime shootings, one is bound to conclude. He was in his bedroom, and Judy had just brought him a plate of cold meat and salad. Once again it was, "Don't get up," the guy walking behind him, the hole blasted into the back of his head, the blood pouring endlessly onto the plate.

When I heard about it, I went over, of course, to see Judy. A month later she sold the house, and I went over again to help her pack things up.

Oh my God, that whole thing of moving. So depressing. The sale of effects. The garage, cleaned. Even the oil stains partially removed by some new process. The books in boxes carried down the stairs—ever so gently, as if they were crates of eggs. I felt a sadness on the stairs as we took down the books as I hadn't really when we'd carried down the corpse.

Carrying the corpse down the stairs, I'd only

thought, Well, he won't be going down *these* stairs again.

JUDY

We went away together and spent the night in a dirty little town way out on the water. The hotels were closed, all the fancy places, the big restaurants—it was the off-season. For whatever reason, we didn't bring anything warm enough to wear, we were both freezing. Well, it was a dark, black, starless, moonless night with gusts of wind banging like fists on the windows of the little inn where we'd finally found a place to stay.

JACK

We walked up a narrow flight of stairs with piles of old towels thrown on the landings. We turned a peculiar bent key in the door.

JUDY

I had to hold on to the doorknob for a moment to keep from fainting. There was no heat in the room at all.

JACK

What about me? I asked. What about me? Did you worry about me when you were away? I was thinking, We already *are* older and wiser. She told me she found my sweater quite nice—very nice colors. I cried a little, then a bit more—dribbling, you know. So love, apparently, was the last thing to go. And I was apparently the last one there to see the end of it. I watched the little flame as it sputtered and spattered, bent its head, and turned into a vague little plume of smoke. Oh well. So that's how it turned out. Who would have guessed. I didn't really want to, but I put my hand around Judy's waist and held her next to me. It was a small gesture which could lead to nothing. My dick lay limply inside my trousers, like a little lunch packed by Mother.

I decided to untie the rope that served me for a belt, and it turned out there was a fireplace there in the room. We made a fire and sat barefoot in front of it.

JUDY

Outside, the wind swept the boardwalk of sand, it swept the porch— And inside our little room I tried to hold him, console him— It was like holding on to a nervous little piglet, he kept slipping away. Meanwhile, some awful trick of the night or the mind made me remember him as he'd once been —his confidence, the warmth, the directness of his touch.

JACK

A burden was lightened now that love was gone. It had always been a difficult word for me.

JUDY

His skin felt like cold clay. I wanted to bathe him, play with him, bring him back to life. But that couldn't happen. Almost all of him was dead.

JACK

In my dream, blue smoke was blowing through the room. The barn door creaked, the cows mooed. I lifted off the ground, feeling very dizzy, dropping ashes faster and faster.

JUDY

The next morning my head was hot—the old symptoms again. As soon as we returned, I put the last of my cartons into a taxi and finally moved out to the apartment I'd found in that very quiet suburb out where Joan lived.

The first thing I did there was to buy some white shirts in the local market, and a pair of sandals. And almost every morning, long before dawn, while it was still pitch-dark, I'd get up, dress, and walk through the little town's empty streets, then down the highway, down to the beach.

Darkness. The sea. The lighthouse. The gulls. The sand thick and wet like black ice cream.

Did I judge you? Sure. I did, of course, but never mind. You'll be forgiven by cooler heads—probably after death, unfortunately, but that's better than never.

The effort people make simply amazes me. Just to get up, get dressed—it's not that easy. To feed oneself, to wash the dishes. I can't believe people do it year after year.

JACK

After the night I saw Judy, as the months passed, I lost my job, but I kept up with my habit of walking through the city. And there was something else that began to happen, where every time that I thought the word "I," it sort of echoed or rang out in my mind, and I was troubled by it. The idea of the self was obsessing me now. What were we all constantly talking about? I didn't get it. The self. The self. What *was* the self? Well, one afternoon, one cloudy, drizzly, late afternoon, I was sitting in my apartment writing in my diary, and unfortunately I'd managed to spill my tea, and my hands were wet, and so was my diary, and my clean laundry, and a bunch of forks, and the clothes I was wearing, and as I reached for a rag and started to wipe things up, I suddenly understood it, very very clearly—and the clarity made me queasy, as if a door had been opened and bright light and oxygen had flooded into my brain. As the rag sat soaking in the tea on my lap, I understood that my self was just a pile of bric-a-brac—just everything my life had quite by chance piled up—everything I'd seen or heard or experienced—meticulously, pointlessly piled up and saved, a heap of nothing, a heap of nothing which had somehow been compressed into some sort of a form and had somehow succeeded in coming alive, and which quite ridiculously now sort of demanded tribute, declared itself great. And the amazing thing was that I'd gone along with it. We all had! We all had bowed down, we all had worshipped, each one kneeling before his own separate self, each apparently obsessed by a single question, a single question to the exclusion of everything: what will happen to this self which is mine? Will "I" achieve magnificence and success? Will "I" be admired? Will my marvelous self express itself? How idiotic! And how boring. How boring, how boring, how boring, how boring. And was this obsession even sincere? Did we honestly feel that no questions but these were of any interest? I wondered if the show of adoration wasn't perhaps just a bit overplayed—whether all the overacting didn't possibly reveal an element of pretense.

And as I thought all this, I felt I saw standing by the window in the fading light that very creature, that self which was mine, that ludicrous figure whom I'd approached till now with such ostentatious displays of respect—such fervor, groveling, hand-kissing and tears—and I went up to the figure, the unpleasant little self, and sort of pulled it by the arm in the fading light, and I spun it around toward me. And then I threw it on its back and kicked it smartly in the face, and then I sat on top of it, grabbed its neck, and choked it and strangled it and bashed its skull against the floor until it stopped squealing, stopped howling, gasped, and was gone.

And what a fucking relief it was. All that endless posturing, the seriousness, the weightiness, that I was so sick sick sick to death of—I'd never have to do any of it ever again.

I would walk the streets like a cheerful ghost, and no one would know my secret. It would really be funny.

And of course I saw immediately all the implications. I could be anything now, whatever I wanted. If I was a ghost, I could walk through walls. It would be so much easier than knocking on doors and begging someone to let me in.

And I thought of something simple to say to people, which they would all understand. I would simply say, "I guess I've always really been a lowbrow at heart."

I guess I've always really been a lowbrow at heart.

So I made a new life, and I was so happy, because it was so easy. I walked down the street with a different step, a sloppier one. I ate in different places, developed different tastes. I'd decided years before what foods I would always say that I didn't like, but I liked them now.

I found a new apartment, and some people might have said it wasn't really very nice. It was smelly, I suppose. But I enjoyed it. There was a window looking out on a courtyard filled with dirt, and children played there—kind of slummy kinds of games.

And you know how I'd always treated books with such respect? I would never even write in a book, or fold down a page, or toss a book casually onto a table. But one morning in my new apartment I did something funny—at least I thought it was funny. I put a book of poetry in the bathtub, and I urinated on it. An interesting experiment. Then I left it in the tub, and then, later, when I needed to shit—I hadn't *planned* this, it just came to me as an idea —instead of shitting into the toilet, I shat on the book. Just to see, you know, if it *could* be done. And apparently it was possible, despite what anyone might have told me. So, like a scientist, I noted in my diary that night, "Yes, the experiment has been a complete success."

My diary, by the way, had a pretty good title. I called it "Experiments in Privacy."

And you know, I'd never been able to stand dogs at all. All the dogs around Howard's house had driven me to the point of paralyzing rage. But it just so happened that I met a boy who was playing in my courtyard, and he gave me his dog, because he was leaving the city, and so the dog moved in with me, and it worked out quite well. We really enjoyed each other, as a matter of fact. But then the dog ran around the wrong corner and got shot, and the sweet little love story came to an end—yes, I guess it came to an end as so many seem to, in a pool of blood. And things got much much quieter after that.

Well, things were shrinking. Things were shrinking for me—everything was shrinking. Sometimes even trying to read the paper, you know, was sort of like spooning food into the mouth of someone who you happen to notice has suddenly died. So actually the thing that became most real, most visible, for me was this little collection of, actually, sex magazines that I'd found one day in a rather nice plastic bag just lying on the street near a puddle. So I spent a lot of time with the somewhat arbitrarily selected group of people who happened to appear in those particular magazines. In fact, I got to know them awfully well—their foibles, whatever—their idiosyncrasies—poses, gestures, expressions, smiles.

And then that too was gone one day. One day it went. I looked at the pictures and got absolutely nothing. I felt nothing. I saw nothing. The pictures were dead. They were paper. They were nothing.

JUDY

One day, inevitably, buying some flowers, I ran into Joan. And so what could she do but invite me to visit? Coffee and buns in her back yard—neat and tidy—but in the brilliant sunshine I couldn't get warm, I felt soaking wet. The nice maid brought out a blanket and draped it carefully across my shoulders.

There was no feeling at all between Joan and me, so I talked about myself. I talked without stopping for two hours about myself, pulling little sounds of understanding out of poor Joan's mouth the way in prison we pulled plates of food from slots in the doors.

God, she was bored. But a few months later she invited me again, and I sat in the kitchen while she cooked a stew. And as she worked away, stirring the big pot, she looked for all the world like a large rodent.

Most evenings, I stayed at home, made some food, played some music. But one night—it was not too long before Joan died—one night I actually ventured into the city, and I went to see a play—*The Stone* by Abromowitz. I must say, I really loved it—and Lars Helbig especially, in the role of the doctor. That whole day I thought about the play. And then the next night, I had dinner with Joan. She'd seen the play the week before and had found it sentimental, and Helbig's acting she'd found very broad. When she said those things, the performance that was sitting in my memory was poisoned. It died. Every moment of it died on contact with her words—every moment's hopeful little face turned purple and died. In the days that followed, it was painful to revisit what had become of the memory I'd had. Finally I emptied the whole evening out of my mind like trash.

JACK

It was one of those weeks when loose ends, apparently, were being tied up. You know, once the people who *do* cause trouble are gone, then it's time to get the ones who *might* cause trouble, or who might once possibly have been *able* to cause trouble twenty years ago—oh, you know the whole story. Eventually it's a matter of tying up loose ends. Tying up loose ends, or cutting them off, is just an inevitable part of the process, obviously. And so, of course, is

the perennial parallel campaign for the betterment
of humanity, or whatever you want to call it, in aid
of which we were being treated now, every week or
so, to demonstrations of a very new approach to
executions, in which eight or ten people would be
taken into a room, seated in these chairs that made
their heads bend way back, and fitted up with
brightly colored tubes in their mouths which sup-
posedly did away with them with very little pain in
this rather odd ceremony—somehow with music or
God knows what. So, anyway, as I sat there in my
apartment one morning, slowly reading in the paper
about this latest attempt to elevate our moral and
esthetic taste, I was looking at one of the photo-
graphs accompanying the article, and I happened
to notice that among the bedraggled-looking people
sitting in those chairs being fitted with tubes were
those rather tiresome moralists whom Howard
found so boring, Tom and Eddie—I quickly scanned
the row for their former friend Martin, until I somehow remembered that he'd recently been appointed
Minister of Supplementary Tugboat Rewiring or

something of the sort—and then I happened to notice that the woman sitting in the very last chair with her head at that rather odd angle was obviously Judy.

Well, I was lost. Where was I? Blinded, you know, like a caught fish jumping about on the floor of a boat. And the funny thing was that aside from sweating and sort of panting—well, more or less exactly as people say when they speak about such moments, I didn't know what to do. I mean, *literally*, what to do—stand up, remain seated, stay in, go out? I reached for my naked friends in the plastic bag, because there they were on the table right next to me. I looked at them all in the midst of their playing, and their hopeful smiles made me wonder if a more compassionate world might not perhaps come about one day. A tiny personal advertisement near one of the pictures asked the unknown reader a simple question: "Have you ever ridden on the train which carries the bodies of the dead?" it inquired disarmingly, and then it commented, "I have, and I was given a berth right next to theirs." There was a postal

box number included, to which you could write to
continue the discussion.

I went out—it was a black afternoon—and I wandered through the streets, oppressed, somehow, by
a terrible sadness. I had an awful feeling of something left undone. Everywhere I went, the leaves had
turned—traitors! I mean, had they no shame? Oh
well, that had been going on, you know, for quite
some time. One noted the usual golds and oranges
and browns amidst the green. I went into the park,
sat on a bench—I seemed to have developed some
variety of what I believe is sometimes called "hysterical" coughing—and then it suddenly hit me that
everyone on earth who could read John Donne was
now dead. They were all dead. And as I turned this
odd fragment of information around in my brain, I
realized that I was the only one left who would even
be aware of the passing of this peculiar group, this
group which was so special, at least in their own
eyes, and my mind went back to a book I'd read
when I was very young about a boy who belonged
to an ancient tribe in a distant land. And in the

course of describing all the customs of the tribe, the book explained that, within the tribe, there were many different sub-groups or clans, and that whenever the last surviving member of one of these clans would die, there would naturally be no one from their family around to mourn them, so then someone who in one way or another had known that last survivor—and if no one was left who had known them well, then it would simply be someone who had known them a little—would be appointed to mourn, publicly, in a sacred spot, the passing of that whole extinguished clan—the designated mourner. And I recalled how the boy in the book had performed that function on a certain occasion, lighting a magnificent sacred fire, weeping and remembering.

I was nervous, queasy, and still weighed down by that odd sadness. Very close by in the center of the park stood that rather dark, cavernous, and always overcrowded café to whose allure all visitors to the park would eventually succumb on even the nicest days, despite the well-known quality of its ambience and food, and I wandered toward it, went in, found a table, and ordered a cup of tea from an overworked waitress. Well, along with the tea, and of her own volition, apparently, or maybe it was the policy of the café's management, the waitress brought me a plate which held a small pastry, a sticky kind of cake whose bottom rested on a bit of paper. And as the waitress left me, I saw my opportunity. First, obviously, I ate the cake. And then I grabbed some matches which sat nearby me, and I glanced around, and I lit the bit of paper. "I am the designated mourner," I said.

The bit of paper wasn't very big, but it burned rather slowly, because of the cake crumbs. I thought I heard John Donne crying into a handkerchief as he fell through the floor—plummeting fast through the earth on his way to Hell. His name, once said by so many to be "immortal," would not be remembered, it turned out. The rememberers were gone, except for me, and I was forgetting: forgetting his name, forgetting him, and forgetting all the ones who remembered him.

A few patrons and waitresses looked over at me irritably until the fire went out. Then I left the place, and I was back in the park.

Would you believe that things were *already* more peaceful? Well, they were, frankly. I could even feel myself breathing more easily and deeply. Everyone I saw looked calmer than before. We all were simply doing much better in every way without the presence on the earth of our nerve-jangling friends, the dear departed mournees, if that's the right word.

I sat once again on the bench I'd been sitting on before. The sun was going down. And I have to say that the colors in the park were quite extraordinary—almost edible, one would have to say. The air was a kind of rose color, and the light which ran through it was a twinkling yellow.

What were we waiting for? The appearance of the Messiah? Was all this nothing? I was quite fed up with the search for perfection. And rather amazed by all that I had—the lemonade stand with its lemonade, the café with its irritable customers and staff, the carousel, the squirrels, the birds, the trees. I'm sorry, Howard, your favorite grove was cut down. But so much remains. This light, so beautiful and warm, was not cut down. The flowers at my feet, with their petals that kiss my ankles like little lips, were not cut down. The trembling air and the trembling sky were not cut down. My sympathy about the loss of your favorite grove is fading out at the end of the day. It said in the paper that there will be fireworks tonight above the carousel, and, right nearby, a parade of young dogs, including some of the newest breeds, some for sale.

I sat on the bench for a very long time, lost—sunk deep—in the experience of unbelievable physical pleasure, maybe the greatest pleasure we can know on this earth—the sweet, ever-changing caress of an early evening breeze.